GEOGRAPHY OF THE WORLD

ASIA

By Deborah Grahame

THE CHILD'S WORLD®
CHANHASSEN, MINNESOTA

The Child's World

Published in the United States of America by The Child's World®
P.O. Box 326, Chanhassen, MN 55317-0326
800-599-READ
www.childsworld.com

Photo Credits: Cover: David Lawrence/Corbis; Animals Animals/Earth Scenes: 11 (Michael S. Bisceglie), 17 (ABPL Image Library), 17 (Michael Fogden), 21 (Jim Steinberg); Corbis: 4 (John Corbett), 5 (Shepard Sherbell), 7 (Jonathan Blair), 9 (Michael S. Yamashita), 14 (Randy Faris), 16 (Alison Wright), 18 (Joe McDonald), 27 (Ben Spencer; Eye Ubiquitous); Picture Desk: 23 (Art Archive/British Museum), 24 (Travelsite/Neil Setchfield).

The Child's World®: Mary Berendes, Publishing Director
Editorial Directions, Inc.: E. Russell Primm, Editorial Director; Pam Rosenberg, Line Editor; Katie Marsico, Assistant Editor; Olivia Nellums, Editorial Assistant; Susan Hindman, Copy Editor; Elizabeth K. Martin, Proofreader; Ann Grau Duvall, Peter Garnham, Carol Yehling, Fact Checkers; Dr. Charles Maynara, Professor of Geography, Radford University, Radford, Virginia, Subject Consultant; Tim Griffin/IndexServ, Indexer; Cian Loughlin O'Day, Photo Researcher; Elizabeth K. Martin, Photo Selector; XNR Productions, Inc., Cartographer

Library of Congress Cataloging-in-Publication Data
Grahame, Deborah A.
  Asia / by Deborah Grahame.
     p. cm. — (Geography of the world series)
Includes index.
Summary: Introduces the geography, topography, and climate of the continent of Asia.
  ISBN 1-59296-058-8 (library bound : alk. paper)
  1. Asia—Geography—Juvenile literature. [1. Asia—Geography.] I. Title. II. Series.
  DS5.92.G73 2003
  915—dc21   2003006339

TABLE OF CONTENTS

CHAPTER ONE

4 Where Is Asia?

CHAPTER TWO

9 How Did Asia Come to Be?

CHAPTER THREE

12 What Makes Asia Special?

CHAPTER FOUR

17 What Animals and Plants Are Found in Asia?

CHAPTER FIVE

22 Who Lives in Asia?

CHAPTER SIX

25 What Is Asia Like Today?

28 Glossary

29 An Asian Almanac

30 Asia in the News

31 How to Learn More about Asia

32 Index

WHERE IS ASIA?

Most of the Asian continent is located in the Northern

Hemisphere. To the west, the Ural and the Caucasus

mountain ranges separate Asia from Europe. Oceans create Asia's

other boundaries. The Bering Strait and the Pacific Ocean border Asia

to the east. Its northern boundary is the Arctic Ocean. The Red Sea

and the Mediterranean Sea are on Asia's southwest coast and the

Indian Ocean is to its south. The Asian main-

land ranges from 77° north **latitude** to

11° south latitude and from 26° east

longitude to 169° west longitude.

Asia stretches from the Arctic in the

north to the Tropics in the south. The most

*Nentsy tribespeople live in the difficult,
snowy conditions of Siberia.*

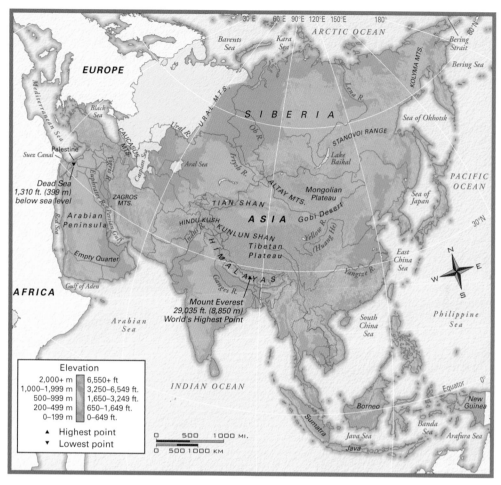

A physical map of Asia

northern part of Asia is Siberia. Siberia is a large region in Russia and

northern Kazakhstan. Siberia is located close to the North Pole. The

most southern part of Asia is the country of Indonesia, which is made

up of a number of islands in Southeast Asia. The continent's tropical

rain forests are located near the **equator.**

ISLAND NATIONS

Japan is located about 100 miles east of Asia's mainland. It is an archipelago, or group of islands. Thousands of islands make up Japan. The Japanese call their country *Nippon,* which means, "Land of the Rising Sun."

Indonesia is also an archipelago. It is made up of more than 17,000 islands. The Philippines is another group of islands—7,000 of them form this country. This archipelago is located northeast of Indonesia.

The **international date line** runs through the Pacific Ocean. The date line is a time zone boundary. There are 11 time zones across Asia. This means that when it is afternoon in Saudi Arabia, it is early morning of the next day in Japan. The continental United States and Canada have only six time zones.

There are 50 Asian countries. Some of the largest and smallest countries in the world are located in Asia. Russia is the world's largest country. It covers an area of 6,592,812 square miles (17,075,383 square kilometers). Bahrain, Singapore, and Maldives are some of the world's smallest countries. Each of them covers an area of less than 300 square miles (777 sq km).

*The Suez Canal in Egypt connects the Mediterranean Sea to the Red Sea
and is one of the major man-made wonders of civilization.*

Asia's borders are close to a few neighboring continents. For this

reason, Asia shares some countries with other continents. Part of Asia

borders with Europe, and two countries— Russia and Turkey—are

located on both continents. Asia is also close to Africa. The Suez

WHAT IS EURASIA?

Some countries seem to be part of both Europe and Asia. These continents share the same landmass. On the west, mountains and seas form the borders that separate the continents of Europe and Asia. Geographers do not all agree on these borders. Some consider Europe a peninsula of Asia. They call the combined continents Eurasia.

Canal, completed in 1869, separates Asia from Africa. Both continents share the country of Egypt.

Because Asia is so large, the climate varies greatly from north to south. In the north, Asia's lower layers of land are frozen all year long. Fertile soil and natural resources are found in East Asia. Central Asia is mainly made up of deserts, **plateaus,** and mountains. The land here is poor for farming. The Himalayas are located in South Asia. To the south of these mountains, the land is fertile. Southeast Asia is a tropical region with rich farmland, forests, and mineral resources. Southwest Asia consists of a desert region in the south and mountains and plateaus in the north. Oil is plentiful in Southwest Asia.

CHAPTER TWO

How Did Asia Come to Be?

Continents are huge landmasses. Scientists believe that millions

of years ago there was only one landmass surrounded by one

ocean. Over time, this supercontinent separated to become the seven

*Scientists think the rocky coast of Minamata Bay in Japan was formed
by volcanic eruptions and lava building up from the ocean floor.*

continents we know today—Africa, Antarctica, Asia, Australia, Europe, North America, and South America. Asia is the largest continent on Earth. The continents of North America and South America together could fit inside the huge continent of Asia.

Continents rest on pieces of the Earth's crust known as tectonic plates. These plates move and shift around all the time. Their edges push and rub against each other. This happens deep under Earth's surface. Over millions of years, there were many small and large plate movements. These movements caused the continents to break away from the first landmass. Asia rests on the oldest and largest tectonic plate.

When powerful movements of Earth's plates caused an earthquake in Taiwan, man-made structures were destroyed in minutes.

Most of the time, these movements are really small. People do not feel them. When a big movement occurs, earthquakes, volcanoes, and tidal waves can result. In Asia, these big plate movements caused many natural wonders.

THE INDIAN SUBCONTINENT

The nation of India makes up most of the subcontinent of India. Off the southern coast of India lies the island nation of Sri Lanka. Off the western coast are the islands of Maldives. The rest of the subcontinent includes Pakistan, Nepal, Bangladesh, and Bhutan. The Himalayas link the Indian subcontinent to the rest of Asia.

CHAPTER THREE

WHAT MAKES ASIA SPECIAL?

Asia is where you will find some of the most special places on

Earth. The continent is home to huge mountain ranges that form

many of the borders of Asia's regions and countries. The Himalayas are

the world's highest mountain range.

Asia also has vast deserts. The Gobi Desert is one of the world's

largest. The Gobi stretches across Mongolia into China. It is not a

sandy desert. Instead, it is made up of gravel and rock. In Saudi Arabia,

a desert called the Empty Quarter is the world's largest body of sand.

Great plateaus are another feature found in Asia. The largest

plateau in the world is the Tibetan Plateau. Much of this plateau is

about 15,000 feet (4,572 meters) above sea level. Because of its high,

large plateau, Tibet is sometimes called the Roof of the World.

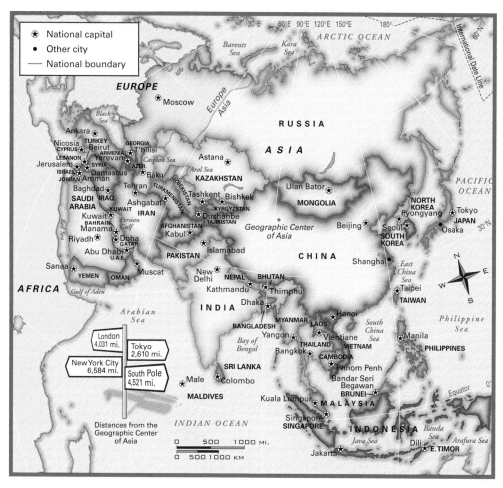

A political map of Asia

Many active volcanoes can be found in Asia. Japan alone has

75 active volcanoes. Along with the Philippines and New Guinea,

Japan is part of the "Ring of Fire." This is a band of active volcanoes

that form a partial circle in the Pacific Ocean.

There are many special bodies of water in Asia. Russia is home to

*Formed from 25 to 30 million years ago, Lake Baikal in Russia
is the oldest and deepest freshwater lake in the world.*

Lake Baikal, the world's deepest lake. This lake is more than one mile

deep in some places. It is also the world's oldest lake. It has existed for

more than 25 million years.

Asia shares the world's largest saltwater lake with Europe. The

Caspian Sea is called a sea, but it is really a salt lake. It lies to the east

of the Caucasus Mountains. This lake is just about the size of

Montana! It covers an area of 143,550 square miles (371,800 sq km).

The longest river in Asia is the Yangtze in East Asia. It is 3,960 miles (6,380 km) long. In Chinese, the name of this river means "long river." The Yangtze River begins in the highlands of Tibet. It flows across China and empties into the East China Sea.

China's other major river is the Yellow River. It is the world's muddiest river. The river is known to the Chinese as "China's Sorrow." This is because the Yellow River has flooded the land many times over the centuries. The floods have taken many lives and destroyed homes and crops.

THE GREAT WALL OF CHINA

The first parts of this famous structure were built in the 3rd century B.C. Over 4,000 miles (6,437 km) long, it is one of the largest construction projects ever carried out. The wall runs near the northern border of China, from a gulf of the Yellow Sea east of Beijing to the southern edge of the Mongolian plain. The wall protected the Chinese from enemies who wanted to invade their land.

*Hindus bathe in the Ganges River because they
believe it has healing and religious powers.*

Hindu people in India consider the

Ganges River the holiest of rivers. They

bathe in the river as part of their religious

beliefs. It is said that the Ganges once flowed through heaven before

the gods sent it to Earth.

CHAPTER FOUR

WHAT ANIMALS AND PLANTS ARE FOUND IN ASIA?

There are plenty of unusual animals in Asia. Many are found

nowhere else. Also, plants and crops that grow in Asia

are important to people around the world.

Giant pandas live in central China.

The bamboo trees they love to eat are

*Fewer than 1,000 giant pandas still live in the wild. The canopy of
a Malaysian rain forest, top right, is home to many rare species.*

plentiful there. The panda may become extinct, however, because its natural habitat is at risk. The Komodo dragon roams a few tiny islands in eastern Indonesia. It is the oldest and largest type of lizard in the world. Gazelles leap in the hilly southwest regions of Asia. Snow leopards prowl the mountains and plateaus of Central Asia.

A snow leopard crouches, ready to pounce.

The vast continent of Asia features several different **biomes.** Each of Earth's biomes has certain weather and land features. Different kinds of plants and animals live in each biome.

The northernmost region of Asia is a **tundra.** There are no trees here. Instead, mosses and short grasses grow in this cold region. Northern Siberia lies on Asia's tundra. Animals that live here include snowy owls and reindeer.

Just south of this region, where the tundra ends, the **taiga** begins. Most of Siberia and northern Russia are in the taiga region of Asia. Spruce and fir trees fill this region. Animals on the taiga include moose and red squirrels.

Lush plants and flowers grow in Southeast Asia's tropical rain forests. The soil here does not hold many nutrients. Instead, the nutrients are stored in the **vegetation.** Asian elephants, parrots, orangutans, and snakes live among the layers of the rain forest.

Short grasses grow in Asia's hot, dry desert regions. The countries of the Arabian Peninsula are in this region. Camels, lizards, gazelles, and wild cats roam here.

Many different crops can be grown in Asia's varied climates. Most of the world's tea and rice are grown in Asia. China grows more cotton than any other country in the world. China and India are the world's top growers of rice. Rice is grown in water-flooded fields called

paddies. Wheat is also widely

grown throughout Asia. It is a

common crop in northeast

China, which is similar in cli-

mate to Kansas in the United

States. China, India, and Russia

are Asia's top wheat producers.

Tea grown on this estate in the Cameron Highlands of Malaysia will be sold around the world.

Sugarcane is another important crop

in Asia. India is the world's number-two producer of sugarcane. The

country of Brazil, in South America, ranks first.

In the deserts of Southwest Asia, olive trees and date palm trees

grow. In parts of South Asia and Southeast Asia, tea bushes, rubber

trees, and nutmeg trees do well in the moist, warm climate. Tea plan-

tations are found mostly in India, China, Sri Lanka, and Indonesia.

CHAPTER FIVE

WHO LIVES IN ASIA?

Many early **civilizations** began in Asia. **Fossils** of early humans have been found throughout the continent. Modern humans may have lived in China more than 20,000 years ago.

Today, people of many cultures and nationalities live on the huge continent of Asia. Each of Asia's regions has several ethnic groups living together. An ethnic group is a group of people with a common language, ancestry, religion, or tradition. Asia's largest ethnic groups are the Chinese and the Arab peoples.

Today, most of Earth's people—almost 4 billion—live in Asia. Some of the world's

ANCIENT ASIA

Important early settlements appeared in ancient Asia. People settled in the great river valleys of Asia, such as the Tigris-Euphrates valley of Mesopotamia, about 3500 B.C. In northwest India, people settled near the Indus River valley about 2500 B.C. People may have settled near the valleys of the Yellow and Yangtze Rivers of north and central Asia around 5000 B.C.

This depiction of Sumerian people, called the Standard of Ur, was created more than 4,000 years ago in what is now the country of Iraq.

THE SHERPA PEOPLE

The Sherpas, an ethnic group found in Tibet and Nepal, farm the land and herd animals. They know the Himalayas well. Sherpas often serve as guides and carriers for mountain climbers. *Sherpa* means "man from the east."

most populated countries are in Asia.

China is home to more people than any other nation in the world. More than 1 billion people live in China. India also has more than 1 billion people. It is the world's second most populated country.

Asia has plenty of land. But many places in Asia are too cold, too hot, too dry, or too mountainous for people to live in. Instead, most

Asian people have settled along coastal areas, or in river or mountain valleys. In some parts of Asia, such as Japan, eastern China, and Bangladesh, people crowd into the cities. Over 16 million people live in Shanghai, China's largest city. This is also China's major port. *Shanghai* means "on the water." China's capital city, Beijing, is home to about 13 million people.

Shanghai, like many other Asian cities such as Bombay and Tokyo, is packed with people.

CHAPTER SIX

WHAT IS ASIA LIKE TODAY?

Since the 1980s, business and industry have increased greatly in Asia. Many people looking for work have moved from the countryside to the cities. Finding a place to live in the city, however, is

> **DOWN TO BUSINESS**
>
> Hong Kong is an island located off the coast of China. The British controlled the island for 155 years. In 1997, Britain returned Hong Kong to the Chinese. It is one of the world's important centers of business.

difficult. Apartments can be tiny and expensive. There are many large cities in Asia today. These cities are crowded with people and cars. Traffic is always a problem. Air pollution is also on the rise.

The influence of Western countries on the countries of Asia has grown stronger over the years. In Japan, this influence is particularly strong. There is a Disneyland in Tokyo, Japan's capital city, and Universal Studios has opened a theme park in Osaka, Japan.

Asia is the birthplace of the world's major religions. Judaism began in Palestine about 2000 B.C. Hinduism began in India about 1500 B.C. Buddhism began there around 500 B.C. Christianity began in Palestine around A.D. 30. Islam began in Arabia about A.D. 610.

If you lived in China today, you would eat very little meat. This is because there is not enough space to raise animals. Most of the land in China is used for growing crops, such as wheat, rice, and vegetables. In Hindu parts of India, beef is never put on the table for dinner. This is because cows are sacred in the Hindu religion. They roam the city streets of Hindu areas freely. Rice is a staple, or an important food, in many Asian countries. In Japan, you would eat plenty of rice, as well as fish. Beef is also available now in Japan.

Strong weather patterns are a fact of life in Asia. Monsoons are winds that bring cold, dry weather in winter. In summer, they bring hot, humid weather. Monsoons can cause floods during the season of heavy rain, between April and October. It can rain steadily for up to four months at a time. Typhoons also blow through parts of Asia regularly. These are strong storms with plenty of hard rain and winds. Tsunamis are huge waves caused by offshore earthquakes. Tsunamis have caused loss of life and serious damage in Asia.

Deforestation has put Asia's forests at risk. Trees of the rain forest are being cut down rapidly. Some trees are cut down for their valuable wood. Other trees are cut and burned for fuel. Some forests are cleared for grazing animals and for farming.

Asia is a land of many contrasts. Its people continue to honor their ancient cultures as they work to meet the challenges of the future. They can take pride in living in a continent with a rich history and many natural wonders.

The heavy rains of the summer monsoon season in India can last from April to September and provide 80 percent of the region's precipitation.

Glossary

biomes (BY-omz) Biomes are ecological communities, such as deserts and rain forests, that support certain types of plant and animal life.

civilizations (siv-ih-luh-ZAY-shuhns) Civilizations are groups of people with a well-developed society, technology, and culture.

deforestation (dee-for-is-TAY-shuhn) Deforestation is the process of clearing land by cutting or burning down forests.

equator (i-KWAY-tur) The equator is an imaginary line that circles Earth halfway between the North and South Poles.

fossils (FOSS-uhls) Fossils are the remains of plants and animals from millions of years ago.

hemisphere (HEM-uhss-fihr) One half of a sphere, such as the northern half or southern half of Earth when it is divided in two by the equator, is called a hemisphere.

international date line (in-tur-NASH-uh-nuhl DAYT LINE) The international date line is an imaginary line on Earth's surface that runs from the North Pole to the South Pole along the 180th meridian (longitude). The line separates one calendar day from the next.

latitude (LAT-uh-tood) Latitude is the position of a place on the globe as it is measured in degrees north or south of the equator.

longitude (LON-juh-tood) Longitude is the position of a place on the globe as it is measured in degrees east or west of an imaginary line known as the prime meridian. The prime meridian runs through the Greenwich Observatory in London, England, and is sometimes called the Greenwich Meridian.

peninsula (puh-NIN-suh-luh) A peninsula is a piece of land that sticks out from a larger piece of land and is almost completely surrounded by water.

plateaus (plah-TOHS) Plateaus are raised, flat areas of land.

sea level (SEE LEV-uhl) Sea level is the average level of the surface of the sea. Measurements of height or depth use sea level as a starting point.

subcontinent (suhb-KON-tuh-nuhnt) A subcontinent is an area of land that is part of a continent but geographically or politically separate.

taiga (TY-guh) The taiga is a biome just below the Arctic region, marked by evergreen forests.

tundra (TUHN-druh) The tundra is a biome in arctic regions where no trees grow and the soil under the ground is permanently frozen.

vegetation (vej-uh-TAY-shuhn) Vegetation is the plant life that covers a certain area.

An Asian Almanac

Location on the Globe:
Longitude: 26° east to 169° west
Latitude: 77° north to 11° south

Greatest distance from north to south: 5,400 miles (8,690 km)

Greatest distance from east to west: 6,000 miles (9,700 km)

Borders: Arctic Ocean, Pacific Ocean, Indian Ocean, Mediterranean Sea, Black Sea, Europe, Bering Strait, Suez Canal, Bosporus Strait, Dardanelles Strait

Total Area: 16,992,000 square miles (44,008,000 sq km)

Highest Point: Mount Everest 29,035 feet (8,850 m) above sea level

Lowest Point: Dead Sea Shore 1,310 feet (399 m) below sea level

Number of Countries on the Continent: 50

Major Mountain Ranges: Altai, Elburz, Himalaya, Hindu Kush, Karakoram, Kunlun, Qilian, Qin Ling, Stanovoy, Tian Shan, Yablonovyy, Zagros

Major Deserts: Gobi, Karakum, Kyzylkum, Rub al Khali, Taklimakan

Major Rivers: Amur, Brahmaputra, Euphrates, Ganges, Huang, Indus, Irrawaddy, Lena, Mekong, Menam, Ob, Salween, Tigris, Xi, Yangtze, Yenisey

Major Lakes: Caspian Sea, Lake Baikal, Lake Balkhash, Aral Sea, Dead Sea

Major Cities:
Mumbai (Bombay), India
Seoul, South Korea
Karachi, Pakistan
Delhi, India
Shanghai, China
Jakarta, Indonesia
Moscow, Russia
Istanbul, Turkey
Tokyo, Japan
Beijing, China
Teheran, Iran
Bangkok, Thailand

Languages: Languages from all major language families except African languages are spoken in Asia.

Population: 3,751, 698,000 (estimated 2000)

Religions: Hinduism, Islam, Buddhism, Confucianism, Taoism, Shinto, Christianity, Judaism

Mineral Resources: Oil, tin, antimony, tungsten, manganese, mica, chromite

Asia in the News

9000 B.C.	Southwest Asians begin to cultivate grains and domesticate animals.
7000 B.C.	Southeast Asians begin to cultivate rice.
5000 B.C.	Mesopotamia begins forming in the Tigris-Euphrates Valley.
3500 B.C.	Sumerians develop the world's first form of writing, known as cuneiform.
2300s B.C.	Sargon of Akkad, a Semitic king, conquers Sumer and unites all of Mesopotamia.
1792 – 1750 B.C.	King Hammurabi rules Babylonia and develops the first set of laws, known as Hammurabi's Code.
1700s B.C.	The widespread Indus civilization gradually breaks apart and is destroyed.
1029 B.C.	The Hebrews establish a kingdom in what is now Israel.
700s B.C.	The Assyrians conquer large parts of southwest Asia.
550 B.C.	The Persian conquest of Babylonia, Palestine, Syria, and all of Asia Minor begins.
326 B.C.	Alexander the Great invades northwest India.
221 B.C.	Construction begins on the Great Wall of China and is completed in A.D. 1500.
A.D. 320	The Gupta dynasty begins in northern India.
636 – 651	Muslim armies invade and take over Syria, Persia, and Egypt.
1206 – 1227	Genghis Khan begins his conquest of Asia and ultimately rules two continents.
1275 – 1292	Italian explorer Marco Polo travels throughout China.
1500s	European traders and Christian missionaries flock to Japan.
1858	The French begin their colonization of Vietnam.
1894 – 1895	Japan wins control of Korea in the Sino-Japanese War.
1985	Economic problems grip the Soviet Union and it begins losing its position as a world power.
1991	The Soviet Union is dissolved.
2003	A new virus emerges causing an outbreak of Severe Acute Respiratory Syndrome (SARS) that begins in China and quickly spreads to other parts of the world.

How to Learn More about Asia

At the Library

Behnke, Alison. *China in Pictures.* Minneapolis: Lerner Publications, 2003.

Gray, Shirley Wimbish. *The Philippines.* New York: Children's Press, 2003.

Gray, Shirley Wimbish. *Vietnam.* New York: Children's Press, 2003.

Hill, Valerie. *Ask about Asia.* Broomall, Penn.: Mason Crest Publishing, 2003.

Hill, Valerie. *India.* Broomall, Penn.: Mason Crest Publishing, 2003.

Hill, Valerie. *Japan.* Broomall, Penn.: Mason Crest Publishing, 2003.

Kazem, Halima. *Afghanistan.* Milwaukee, Wis.: Gareth Stevens, 2002.

Nickles, Greg. *Russia, the Land.* New York: Crabtree Publishing Company, 2000.

On the Web

Visit our home page for lots of links about Asia:

http://www.childsworld.com/links.html

Note to Parents, Teachers, and Librarians: We routinely verify our Web links to make sure they're safe, active sites—so encourage your readers to check them out!

Places to Visit or Contact

ASIA SOCIETY

To write for information about the many countries and cultures of Asia

725 Park Avenue
New York, NY 10021
212/288-6400

THE FIELD MUSEUM

To tour their permanent exhibits on the many cultures and environments found in Asia

1400 South Lake Shore Drive
Chicago, IL 60605
312/922-9410

Index

animal life, 17–18, 20, 26
Arab culture, 22
Arabian Peninsula, 20
Arctic Ocean, 4
Arctic region, 4–5

Beijing, China, 24
Bering Strait, 4
biomes, 19

Caspian Sea, 14–15
Caucasus Mountains, 4, 14
China, 12, 15, 17, 20–21,
    22, 23, 24, 25, 26
climate, 8, 20, 23, 26

deforestation, 27
deserts, 8, 12, 20

East China Sea, 15
economy, 25
Empty Quarter, 12
ethnic groups, 22

farming, 8, 20–21, 26
floods, 15, 26–27
foods, 26

Ganges River, 16

giant pandas, 17–18
Gobi Desert, 12

Himalaya Mountains, 8
Hinduism, 16, 26

Indian Ocean, 4
Indonesia, 6
International date line,

Japan, 13, 25

Komodo dragon, 18

Lake Baikal, 14

Mediterranean Sea, 4
monsoons, 26–27
mountains, 4, 8, 12, 18

natural resources, 8

Osaka, Japan, 25

Pacific Ocean, 4
plant life, 17, 19, 20, 27
plateaus, 8, 12
population, 23, 24

rain forests, 5
Red Sea, 4
religion, 16, 26
rice paddies, 21
"Ring of Fire," 13
rivers, 15–16
Russia, 5, 6, 7, 13–14, 19, 21

Shanghai, China, 24
Siberia, 5, 19
Singapore, 6
Suez Canal, 7–8

taiga region, 19
tectonic plates, 10–11
Tibetan Plateau, 12
Tokyo, Japan, 25
Tropics region, 5, 8, 20
tsunamis, 27
tundra region, 19
typhoons, 27

Ural Mountains, 4

volcanoes, 13

Yangtze River, 15
Yellow River, 15

About the Author

Deborah Grahame writes and edits children's books at her office near Candlewood Lake in Connecticut. From an early age, Deborah has been fascinated by Asian art, culture, and philosophy. One of her favorite Asian foods is miso soup. Her favorite Asian writer is the Sufi poet Rumi. This photo was taken on a snowy, springtime afternoon at the Chuang Yen Monastery in Carmel, New York, not far from her home.